Mat Time
Devotions to Enrich Your Martial Arts Classes

By: Ginny Tyler

ISBN: 978-1-7336151-1-2

Glory to God, who is able to do far beyond all that we could ask or imagine by his power at work within us.

Ephesians 3:20

Testimonials

"Ginny Tyler has written an extremely useful guide for martial arts instructors who want to share Christian concepts with their students. She has combined Scripture verses along with insights right out of martial practice. I cannot recommend this enough for Bible believing black belt teachers for use in their classes or even just for their own personal devotions."

Keith D. Yates
Chairman of the Board of Governors, Gospel Martial Arts Union
President, American Karate and Tae Kwon Do Organization

"*Mat Time* is a great addition to the Christian exposition for young martial arts students and their instructors. Another blessing from the Lord through the author of the *Kingdom Kicks* series."

Michael Proctor
10th Dan, Renbudo
Board Member of the GMAU
Martial Arts Professional at the Cooper Aerobics Center

Day 1: Spiritual Blocking

Key verse(s): Ephesians 6:13-18
"Therefore put on the full armor of God, so that when the day of evil comes, you may be able to stand your ground, and after you have done everything, to stand. Stand firm then, with the belt of truth buckled around your waist, with the breastplate of righteousness in place, and with your feet fitted with the readiness that comes from the gospel of peace. In addition to all this, take up the shield of faith, with which you can extinguish all the flaming arrows of the evil one. Take the helmet of salvation and the sword of the Spirit, which is the word of God. And pray in the Spirit on all occasions with all kinds of prayers and requests. With this in mind, be alert and always keep on praying for all the Lord's people."

Have you ever thought about the importance of blocking? We have many types of blocks that move upward, downward, inside, and outside, but they are all designed to do the same thing. Blocks are intended to protect our bodies from physical harm that comes from an opponent.

What would happen if we did not block an attack? We would get hit! And how long could we fight off an attacker if we were injured? Probably not very long.

In the same way, we need to understand that it is just as important to "block" our spirits from spiritual attacks.

Ephesians 6:16 says, "In addition to all this, take up the shield of faith, with which you can extinguish all the flaming arrows of the evil one." You see, it is just as important to protect our spiritual side from sin and offenses from "the evil one" as it is to protect our physical bodies from the opponent in front of us.

So, the next time you are training your body to defend attacks that may come your way, remember the attacks that you often do not see until it is too late. The time to prepare for those unseen attacks is now. Fortify your defenses, get in the Word, and sharpen your sword of the spirit. For it is not a matter of "if" the fiery arrows come raining down — it is "when."

Use the space below to add your thoughts, experiences, and convictions to make this message more personal for your audience.

Day 2: Balance Check!

Key verse(s): Matthew 7:24-27

"Therefore everyone who hears these words of mine and puts them into practice is like a wise man who build his house on the rock. The rain came down, the streams rose, and the winds blew and beat against that house; yet it did not fall, because it had its foundation on the rock. But everyone who hears these words of mine and does not put them into practice is like a foolish man who built his house on the sand. The rain came down, the streams rose, and the winds blew and beat against that house, and it fell with a great crash."

In this parable, Jesus is explaining to his audience the importance of not only hearing His instruction, but also being doers of it. He compares the doer of the word to a man who built his house on a rock, while the ones who listen only are building a foundation on the sand. As you read in the parable, the rock of Christ is a firm foundation that does not allow the house to be shaken, while the house on the sand crumbles when the storms rage.

In our martial arts classes, we learn that stances are very important. So important, in fact, that it is often one of the first things that you all learn. Why is that?

Because people who have studied the martial arts for a very long time understand that how stable someone's stance is can be the difference between victory and defeat. It can not only hold you steady during an attack, but oftentimes, you can also use a really good stance to take down someone else who's stance may not be as firmly planted!

Students, it is very important to have a foundation that is strong enough to support everything else going on above the waist. Try doing a punch, or a kick in a really bad stance. What happens? Furthermore, what happens when you actually hit a target with a faulty stance?

The next time you are working on your stances, remember Matthew 7:25: "The rain came down, the streams rose, and the winds blew and beat against that house; yet it did not fall, because it had its foundation on the rock."

Use the space below to add your thoughts, experiences, and convictions to make this message more personal for your audience.

Day 3: Keep Your Eyes Straight

Key verse(s): Romans 12:2
"Do not conform to the pattern of this world, but be transformed by the renewing of your mind. Then you will be able to test and approve what God's will is – his good, pleasing and perfect will."

When you are practicing your katas, are you ever tempted to sneak a peek at what the student next to you is doing?

Do you ever forget what you are doing and rely on the people around you to know what to do next?

As martial artists, we practice our katas to train our bodies how to react to certain scenarios, how to move in ways we would not know how to otherwise, and to develop a muscle memory that could potentially last a lifetime. (Depending on how much you practice, of course).

But what happens when you look to others to know what to do next? More often than not, you end up following their mistakes blindly, thinking you are doing the right thing. But in reality, it gets you more lost than you were before.

It's interesting to note that the word "kata" means pattern, and in Romans 12:2, the writer Paul is telling us not to conform to the patterns of this world. What does this mean to us as martial artists?

Keep your eyes straight! Don't rely on others to show you what to do next, rather, allow Christ to show you the way. But here's the challenge. To allow Him to do that, you have to get in the Word, learn His teachings, and study them just as much as you study the martial arts. Only then can you be confident in your next steps — only then will you know what you should do both in, and outside of your martial arts classes.

Rather than letting the world around you lead your course of action, allow Jesus to. Unlike the world, He will never lead you astray.

Use the space below to add your thoughts, experiences, and convictions to make this message more personal for your audience.

Day 4: Sensei May I?

Key verse(s): Proverbs 3:27
"Do not withhold good from those to whom it is due, when it is in your power to act."

Have you ever played a game called "mother, may I?" In it, a group of players are trying to see who can make their way to the person at the front of the room by asking politely various requests such as "mother, may I take two steps forward?" or "mother, may I take one hop forward?"

The player at the front of the room has the ability to allow or deny these requests until finally, one person becomes the winner by reaching this leader. What is the point of this game? The players would probably say winning! But the adults know better. This is a great game to reinforce the character trait of courtesy by politely making your requests be known — and not getting upset if the answer is "no."

Courtesy is an amazing character trait, and in the book of Genesis, there is even a story about Abraham showing courtesy to strangers who visited him one day. Rather than nodding them off, he showed courtesy to them, bowing to the ground in front of them, and serving them his table's best. It was after all this that he learned the strangers were angels! Imagine how he would have felt if he had treated them badly and found that out afterwards.

What does courtesy look like in our martial arts classes? We do many things to show courtesy to our instructors like bowing, saying "yes sir" and "yes ma'am", raising our hand before speaking out, and not challenging those of a higher rank.
We also show courtesy to our fellow students by showing them respect, being helpful and encouraging, and by showing kindness.

Proverbs 3:27 tells us not to withhold good when it is in your power to act. My question to you is: are you able to bow? Are you able to speak courteously — saying "please" and "thank you?" Are you able to hold your tongue for your chance to speak? If so, then we are commanded to do just that!

We would be wise to follow in the way of Abraham, showing courtesy to each other, because you never know what blessings will come your way when you do.

Use the space below to add your thoughts, experiences, and convictions to make this message more personal for your audience.

_____

_____

_____

_____

_____

_____

_____

_____

_____

_____

_____

_____

_____

_____

Day 5: Step Right Up!

Key verse(s): 2 Corinthians 12:9-10
"But he said to me, "My grace is sufficient for you, for my power is made perfect in weakness." Therefore I will boast all the more gladly about my weaknesses, so that Christ's power may rest on me. That is why, for Christ's sake, I delight in weaknesses, in insults, in hardships, in persecutions, in difficulties. For when I am weak, then I am strong."

Who has been to a carnival that had a test of strength game? Usually this entails someone trying to hit a specific spot with a mallet to see "how strong" they are. (And usually, it results in someone feeling poorly about themselves as they walk away disappointed in their results)

What about when we spar? Do we usually assume the bigger student, or even the one with the higher rank will always win? Do you have a sense of defeat when you are paired up with someone much bigger than you?

I'll tell you about someone who may have felt the same way as you, but despite the odds, this person relied on a strength much greater than his own. In the book of 1 Samuel, we learn about David, a shepherd boy who agreed to fight Goliath because no one else would. David was young, unarmed, and had only a sling and stones to fight with because when he tried to put armor on and hold a sword, both were too heavy for him to move around! Imagine how disappointed you might feel if you were vulnerable like he was. Now Goliath, he was a trained Philistine soldier, an adult that was around 9 feet tall, AND he had armor and a spear!

The odds weren't looking too good, were they? But guess what? Goliath was banking on his physical strength, while David relied on God's strength. 2 Corinthians 12:9 says that God's power is made perfect in weakness. But what did that look like on the battlefield for David? (I'll give you a hint. After slinging just one stone, David was the victor)

What happened here? David relied on his weakness to allow God's strength to shine through. So next time you feel weak, be happy! That just gives God a chance to move through your actions and victories, and through Him, you can do far more than you would have been able to using your own strength.

Use the space below to add your thoughts, experiences, and convictions to make this message more personal for your audience.

_____

_____

_____

_____

_____

_____

_____

_____

_____

_____

_____

_____

_____

_____

_____

_____

Day 6: I Obey Right Away!

Key verse(s): 1 John 3:24
"The one who keeps God's commands lives in him, and he in them. And this is how we know that he lives in us: We know it by the Spirit he gave us."

Do you ever wonder why there are so many commands in the martial arts? Is there a reason your instructors have so many rules? Why is that??

Obedience is a huge part of being a martial arts student because there are many regulations in place to keep you safe, as well as to teach you character traits that will benefit you for a lifetime.

But did you know there were many times in the Bible where God gave instructions that may not have made any sense at the time, but worked for the benefit of the one who listened and obeyed?
Let's look at a few of these examples:

In the book of Joshua, we learn about how the Israelites came into the promised land, despite a really big wall! God instructed Joshua and the Israelites to march around this wall once a day for 6 days while playing trumpets and carrying the Ark of the Covenant around the city. On the seventh day, they were to march around the wall seven times! These orders probably did not make much sense to them at the time, but on the seventh day, the Israelites finished marching, let out a loud yell, and the walls miraculously fell down!

In the book of Genesis, we learn about Noah, who was given very specific instruction on how to build a REALLY big boat for the rain to come, and everyone thought he was crazy for obeying! But Noah was obedient to instruction, and because of this, he and his family were spared the torrential rains that laid waste to the rest of the earth.

Another example, but by far not the last, is the story of Gideon, found in the book of Judges. Gideon was told by an angel that he was to rescue the Israelites from the hands of Midian, so he raised an army of thousands for the task. Imagine his surprise when God wanted him to lessen his army to a mere 300! Nonetheless, Gideon obeyed, and with the favor of the Lord, he was victorious.

Next time you don't feel like obeying the class rules, remember there is always a reason for them, even if you don't see it right away.

Use the space below to add your thoughts, experiences, and convictions to make this message more personal for your audience.

Day 7: Move On Down

Key verse(s): Luke 14:8-11
"When someone invites you to a wedding feast, do not take the place of honor, for a person more distinguished than you may have been invited. If so, the host who invited both of you will come and say to you, 'Give this person your seat.' Then, humiliated, you will have to take the least important place. But when you are invited, take the lowest place, so that when your host comes, he will say to you, 'Friend, move up to a better place.' Then you will be honored in the presence of all the other guests. For all those who exalt themselves will be humbled, and those who humble themselves will be exalted."

Let's try something different today. I want each of you to take a cup in your hands. Now, if you wanted to fill the cup up, which way would you hold it? Would you keep the open side down, or would you turn it upwards?

Well of course, you would hold the opening up! Otherwise, anything you put into it would fall right out!

Did you realize that cup is an excellent demonstration of our ability to learn with or without humility? You see, if you hold the cup bottom-side up, that is the opposite of a humble spirit — it is a demonstration of pride. Can anything go in? Can knowledge go in? How about growth? What about experience?

Now, turned with the opening facing up, that is a demonstration of a humble spirit. We are able to learn, grow, and fill ourselves with the knowledge and experience that our instructors are sharing with us.

Does it make sense to go to martial arts classes if you *don't* want to learn? (I hope you said "no"). There are so many things we can learn in class, but only if we have the right attitude of humility to receive that information.

In fact, if you look at the key verses for today, this is an excellent demonstration of how we are to line up before and after class each day! Ephesians 4:2 tells us, "Be completely humble and gentle...", and this is not a request, it is a command.

Think about how our Lord and Savior was born? He is the Lord of Lords, and he was born in a lowly stable, then put into an animal manger. Even at birth, Jesus was the perfect example of humility. And in His likeness, we need to try our best to follow His lead.

Use the space below to add your thoughts, experiences, and convictions to make this message more personal for your audience.

Day 8: Don't Back Down

Key verse(s): Daniel 3:16-18
"Shadrach, Meschach and Abednego replied to him, "King Nebuchadnezzar, we do not need to defend ourselves before you in this matter. If we are thrown into the blazing furnace, the God we serve is able to deliver us from it, and he will deliver us from Your Majesty's hand. But even if he does not, we want you to know, Your Majesty, that we will not serve your gods or worship the image of gold you have set up."

Being in the martial arts teaches us something that is easily carried into our lives outside of the dojo walls: indomitable spirit.

In the story above, we read about Shadrach, Meschach, and Abednego, who were threatened with death if they did not worship the idol King Nebuchadnezzar set up. But despite the threat, they refused to do what they knew was wrong in the eyes of God, and they were willing to take the consequence.

Two things Nebuchadnezzar didn't bank on was the power of their faith — and the power of God. Not only were the three men thrown into a furnace heated seven times as hot as it was before — and completely unharmed, but they didn't even smell of smoke when they came out! (The same cannot be said for the guards who threw them in)

Did they know this would happen? Of course not! But still, they demonstrated indomitable spirit because they would not waver on their morals and denounce their God.

What does indomitable spirit look like in the martial arts? It could be fixing your eyes on what you know is right, in and outside of class. Has anyone ever tempted you to use your martial arts for the wrong reason? Has anyone tried to convince you to quit just because it is hard? Has anyone tried to get you to make bad choices, even when you know it was wrong? Guess what? Holding fast to your integrity takes indomitable spirit!

2 Timothy 4:7 tells us, "I have fought the good fight, I have finished the race, I have kept the faith." Will you be able to say the same?

Use the space below to add your thoughts, experiences, and convictions to make this message more personal for your audience.

Day 9: Battle Ready

Key verse(s): Psalm 144:1
"Praise be to the Lord my Rock, who trains my hands for war, my fingers for battle."

Have you ever wondered if it is ok to study the martial arts if you are a Christian? Don't worry, many people have probably wondered the same thing. In fact, if you look at Matthew 5:39, Jesus says "If anyone slaps you on the right cheek, turn to them the other cheek also." This has left Christians wondering for many, many years if training in the martial arts is even permissible.

But if you look at our Bible verse above, the psalmist David credits his ability to fight to God. And if you look throughout the Old Testament, you see many instances where the Israelites were given permission and even commands to fight their enemies. One example is Deuteronomy 7:2: "and when the Lord your God has delivered them over to you and you have defeated them, then you must destroy them totally."

For clarification, let's look at the customs of the culture. The right hand was considered "the clean hand", while the left was "unclean." To strike someone with the clean hand (on the right cheek) is the equivalent of a back slap. This is not a threat of life or an act that would rob you of your livelihood. To offer them the opportunity to then slap the left cheek would force them to use the unclean hand, which was culturally unacceptable and creates problems for the aggressor.

All that to say, a back slap is not the same as an aggressive confrontation. Learning how to defend your and your loved one's lives are two different scenarios, and it is up to us to have the discernment to know when to take the passive approach—and when to defend ourselves.

Would we use our martial arts skills on a friend who called you a name?
How about on a sibling that broke your favorite toy?

I hope not! But what about on a grown-up who was trying to hurt you? That would be an acceptable time. And it is up to you to talk with your instructor on when you should or should not use martial arts when you leave your dojo.

Use the space below to add your thoughts, experiences, and convictions to make this message more personal for your audience.

_____

_____

_____

_____

_____

_____

_____

_____

_____

_____

_____

_____

_____

_____

_____

_____

_____

Day 10: Integrity: Do What Is Right, Even When No One Is Looking

Key verse(s): 1 Samuel 26:23
"The Lord rewards everyone for their righteousness and faithfulness."

Raise your hand if you have ever been tempted to do something that you knew was wrong. What about if a friend tried to coerce you into doing something that went against your morals? (You might have to evaluate if that person really is a friend). If so, you're not alone! Guess what? Temptations come our way throughout our entire lives! But the good news is that we can have as much integrity as we will allow ourselves to have.

Integrity is doing the right thing, even when no one is looking. Let's say you see a classmate drop some money out of their pocket as they are leaving martial arts class—what would you do? How about if you are sparring someone who you know is hurt? Would you take advantage of their weakness, or would you adjust your style so that you both can learn without getting hurt? How about moving up in ranks. Would you work hard to earn a black belt one day-or would you change schools because you know their tests aren't as hard?

All of these things and more take copious amounts of integrity. And these challenges will not go away, however much we want them to. Integrity is something we must ALWAYS carry with us, and it starts with you.

Now, what if you do the right thing, and you don't get a reward right away? Would you still do what is right in the eyes of God?

Did you know… that sometimes our rewards don't come to us on earth? James 1:12 says, "Blessed is the one who perseveres under trial because, having stood the test, that person will receive the crown of life that the Lord has promised to those who love him." Furthermore, Matthew 16:27 says, "For the Son of Man is going to come in his Father's glory with his angels, and then he will reward each person according to what they have done."

Guess what? This means we will probably need patience if we are waiting for that reward. But know this. The rewards you wait for will be so much better than anything you could earn on earth. 1 Corinthians 9:25 promises us "a crown that will last forever." I don't know about you, but I'd rather have something that can't get lost or broken!

Use the space below to add your thoughts, experiences, and convictions to make this message more personal for your audience.

Day 11: Follow The Leader

Key verse(s): 1 Corinthians 11:1
"Follow my example, as I follow the example of Christ."

Do you ever wonder how your instructor came to know *so much* about the martial arts? Some of it is likely their own doing, but chances are, the majority of what they know came from their instructors. Did you know that the Japanese term "sensei" literally means "person born before another", or "one who has gone before." The hidden meaning behind this is that there is someone who started a particular journey before you did and knows more than you do because they have more experience on this symbolic path.

But how does this apply to our Christian walk? The answer really is quite simple, for we all have the One "who has gone before" us, who has modeled perfect love, character, integrity, and approach to life. Do you all know who I am talking about? Jesus!

Much like we are to follow Christ's model of life, in our martial arts classes, we are to model our instructors, for they have so much more experience and wisdom than you likely have. And one day, you may be the instructor, leading other students down the path you have already gone down, sharing your wisdom, technique, experiences, and more with students you hope will do the same one day. But you might wonder, "how will I ever have that much wisdom??" This part is easy, for we all have a perfect instructor that has infinite wisdom.

In John 8:12, Jesus says, "I am the light of the world. Whoever follows me will never walk in darkness, but will have the light of life." As long as we all follow after the Great Teacher, we will never lack lessons that we can pass down to our students (or even try to master ourselves!) And guess what? Just when you think you've learned everything there is to learn, all you have to do is open the Bible and see what God has for you that day.

The lesson in all this is to follow the "patterns" of our instructors – and especially, the Great Instructor. Who is this? (Allow students to answer)

Jesus! That's right! Follow in His ways, and there will always be opportunity for growth in your life.

Use the space below to add your thoughts, experiences, and convictions to make this message more personal for your audience.

Day 12: Don't Give Up

Key verse(s): Galatians 6:9
"Let us not become weary in doing good, for at the proper time we will reap a harvest if we do not give up."

Raise your hand if you think getting a black belt is an easy task? Guess what? It's not! Getting a black belt is really, really hard, and it takes a lot of perseverance to attain one. It takes even more perseverance to keep learning after you get a black belt and to continue to move up in rank. Why is that?

Getting a black belt, like most anything worthwhile, takes a lot of hard work, patience, integrity, flexibility, indomitable spirit, and so many other character traits that we have talked about already. But perseverance ranks at the top. Know why? Because you have to be willing to not give up when you are tired physically. You have to push through long periods of waiting to test. You have to practice—a LOT, sometimes when you would rather be doing something else. You also have to look in your heart to see if you are humble enough to continue learning, or willing to take instruction well.

Though getting your black belt is NOT the end of the line, I do compare the process to running a race. Running is not easy—running long distances is even harder. In Hebrews 12:1, the writer states, "Therefore, since we are surrounded by such a great cloud of witnesses, let us throw off everything that hinders and the sin that so easily entangles. And let us run with perseverance the race marked out for us, fixing our eyes on Jesus, the pioneer and perfecter of faith."

This means that if you want to "finish the race", you have to disregard distractions and keep your eyes straight ahead – whether that is on the goal of earning a black belt one day, or something greater like joining the ranks in Heaven. The bottom line is that anything worthwhile will take time, focus, and perseverance, and you need to be prepared to tackle all of the above if you want to reap an abundant harvest.

Use the space below to add your thoughts, experiences, and convictions to make this message more personal for your audience.

_____

_____

_____

_____

_____

_____

_____

_____

_____

_____

_____

_____

_____

_____

Day 13: First Place!

Key verse(s): Psalms 139:23-24
"Search me, God, and know my heart; test me and know my anxious thoughts. See if there is any offensive way in me, and lead me in the way everlasting."

How many of you have done martial arts tournaments? They can be hard, right? Sometimes they are big tournaments, and you don't know your way around. Then take in to account other schools may be there, and you have to compete against students you have never seen do kata or spar before. You have to keep your wits about you and do your best or you could easily get overrun by your opponent - or yourself.

Wait a minute. Did I say yourself? Yep. Guess what, students? You can be your own greatest opponent.

Sometimes you just keep your eyes on that trophy, and to get it, you would even compromise your morals. Maybe you throw a technique that you know is too rough, or another one that isn't allowed (and you just hope the judges didn't notice). Maybe you get spiteful or rude to another student who beat you, even though you might not have done that any other day.

Tournaments offer a unique opportunity for you to examine yourself. And rather than beating every other student out there, you first have to conquer your own heart. In the book of Psalms, David is asking God to search his heart and to test him, and he goes on to ask God to rid him of any offensive ways.

How often do we ask God to do that in us?

Did you know that all that "stuff" in your heart — you know, the offensive things, the rude things, and the mad things. All of those things will hold you back from being the best "you" that you can be. And ultimately, not being "the best you" could be what stands between you and your goals.

Take a lesson from David and first ask God to help you stay on the path you know you need to be on. Clean your heart of anything dirty so that you can not only set an example for others, but also continue to grow in a way that you would not be able to otherwise.

Use the space below to add your thoughts, experiences, and convictions to make this message more personal for your audience.

Day 14: Watch Yourself!

Key verse(s): Proverbs 16:32
"Better a patient person than a warrior, one with self-control than one who takes a city."

The martial arts is very unique among other athletic avenues in that it offers emphasis on self-control. Why is this? Is it because people can get hurt if they don't exercise it? Of course, that is one reason, but did you know that there are two types of self-control? One type is physical – controlling your body. And the other is internal – controlling your thoughts and feelings. Both of these are essential not only to the martial arts, but also to life itself.

What happens if you are sparring, and your partner has no self-control?
(You might be scared to work with someone like that).

What if you are doing self-defense with a partner, and they execute a move that injures you. No one wants to be on the receiving end of a lack of physical self-control, but equally so, no one wants to be with a partner that can't control their emotions either.

Proverbs 25:28 tells us, "Like a city whose walls are broken through is a person who lacks self-control." Did you know that not being able to control your emotions also makes you weaker? We've all heard that in cases of sparring where one person is just so angry that they can't think straight and end up losing the match. But what about other choices? If you really like cookies and chips and lack self-control, you may fill up on the bad stuff so much you don't have room for nutritious food, and your body will suffer. Or what if you surround yourself with bad company and don't exercise self-control when they tempt you to do something that can get you into trouble? How about if you get angry in school and yell at your classmates – or even a teacher? All of these poor choices, and more, only weaken you physically, spiritually, and emotionally.

It is up to all of you to exercise your self-control muscle so that you can stay healthy inside and out, and this, ultimately, will lead to a greater outcome today and in your adult lives.

Use the space below to add your thoughts, experiences, and convictions to make this message more personal for your audience.

Day 15: Using Your Gifts

Key verse(s): 1 Corinthians 12:4-6
"There are different kinds of gifts, but the same Spirit distributes them. There are different kinds of service, but the same Lord. There are different kinds of working, but in all of them and in everyone it is the same God at work."

Have you ever practiced kata with your classmates, and everyone was perfectly timed on their moves, yells, and finishes? It's pretty amazing to see, isn't it? (Of course, you shouldn't be looking around too much). But this doesn't happen too often because usually you have people who are better at kata than others, or have better timing. In the same way, you may have some classmates that are better at sparring than you are, or perhaps you are better at self-defense than others. Why is that? Why can't you all be the same?

1 Corinthians 12:4-6 reminds us that we all have different gifts, given to us by God, but it is the same power of God that works in all of us. What would happen if all of us had the same talents and shortcomings? There would not be much room for growth.

Fast forward in 1 Corinthians 12 to verse 12, and Paul tells us, "Just as a body, though one, has many parts, but all its many parts forms one body, so it is with Christ." What does this mean? No one body can be made of arms, right? That would look awfully weird. Or what if we were composed of all eyes. Sure, we could see great, but how would we move? God made our bodies to have many parts so that each one could specialize in a different task to work together with the body so that it could grow and thrive. And guess what? We're the same way.

You may have fellow classmates that struggle in a certain area of martial arts that you excel in. That's an opportunity for you to reach out and help them. In the same way, they may be helping you one day with something you are falling short on.

Much like the body of Christ, our martial arts classes are filled with people who have different talents, experiences, and abilities. Next time you are tempted to laugh when someone makes a mistake, remember that you can't all be toes or hands, or even hearts. It takes all parts for the body to work the way God intended.

Use the space below to add your thoughts, experiences, and convictions to make this message more personal for your audience.

Day 16: Training For The Ultimate Prize

Key verse(s): 1 Timothy 4:7-8
"Have nothing to do with godless myths and old wives' tales; rather, train yourself to be godly. For physical training is of some value, but godliness has value for all things, holding promise for both the present life and the life to come."

How many of you practice your martial arts at home, throughout the week, as well as in class? Now, how many of you do the same when you are getting ready for a test?

The truth is, it is important to train all the time, whether you are preparing for a test or not, but I'm not talking about physical training. Well, there is that too, but spiritual training should never take a break. Why is that? Because our spiritual muscles are in just as much need of training as every other part of our body, and as our key verse explains above, it is more imperative to train the spirit than the body!

We may be in tip top shape now, but one day, we will begin to slow down physically. There will only be so much we can do when we are older as we lose some of our flexibility and strength. Our spiritual muscles, on the other hand, can only continue to get stronger as we train them, regardless of our age. In fact, we need those muscles not only for this life, but for the life to come as well—and that one lasts forever.

How do we train our spiritual muscles? Just as we push ourselves past physical comfort, we need to test our boundaries spiritually as well. Read the Bible every day, reach out and offer help to others, whether they like us or not. Share the Gospel, regardless of how we think the person will react. Stand your ground when it comes to principles, and seek the Lord ceaselessly with thanksgiving and praise, regardless of what is going on in our lives. Does that seem challenging to you? It does to me! But that should not dissuade us from pushing ourselves more than we think we can go because the fruits of those efforts will be more rewarding than you could imagine.

Just remember that if you find yourself staying in your comfort zone all the time, you will never branch out the way God knows you can if you just trust Him with your comfort and press forward towards your eternal prize.

Use the space below to add your thoughts, experiences, and convictions to make this message more personal for your audience.

Day 17: Say What?

Key verse(s): James 1:19
"My dear brothers and sisters, take note of this: Everyone should be quick to listen, slow to speak, and slow to become angry, because human anger does not produce the righteousness that God desires."

Now, I want you all to think about today's key verse while I talk because just by listening to what I say, we will be demonstrating today's topic!

Why is it important to be quick to listen and slow to speak? (Please raise hands and wait for me to call on you before speaking).

Have your parents ever told you something that was really important? How about your instructors in this martial arts class? Have you ever been told something that could be dangerous if you *didn't* listen?

Here's a few scenarios, because the point I want to make is that paying attention could be the difference between a safe and an unsafe situation. I'll go through a few commands, and you tell me if each one could be dangerous if you weren't paying attention:

- Do not cross the road before looking for cars
- Do not start kicking until I tell you to begin
- The stove is hot so do not touch it
- Bedtime is at 8:00 PM
- Keep your punches towards the target, not the person next to you
- Line up at the end of class

As you can see, some of these things are not as imperative, but the others are so important that you could be dangerously hurt if you are not quick to listen. For some of them, maybe you don't get hurt, but another person does, which brings up a new point. For the safety of you and those around you, you would be wise to first listen, and then speak.

When you all go home tonight, I want you to give your family an extra dose of attentiveness and be sure to pay attention both at home, and in this classroom.

Use the space below to add your thoughts, experiences, and convictions to make this message more personal for your audience.

Day 18: Prepare For Battle

Key verse(s): Ephesians 6:12
"For our struggle is not against flesh and blood, but against the rulers, against the authorities, against the powers of this dark world and against the spiritual forces of evil in the heavenly realms."

In our martial arts classes, we primarily learn how to do battle with physical opponents. Sparring partners, imagined bad guys, pretend attackers, and the like. But do you ever stop to think about how you are going to fight your spiritual battles?

What is a spiritual battle? You may not notice many of them when you are a kid, but as you get older, you start to realize that most challenges in life come from outside factors, rather than physical people in front of you. These challenges can come in the form of loss, temptation to sin, anger, seasons of sickness, and so much more. While we want to avoid these hardships, they are, unfortunately, a part of life until we join Jesus in Heaven.

Does that mean we have no choice in the impact these seasons have in us? Does this mean we are always easy prey to the enemy, just waiting around to be attacked? Not at all! In fact, the Bible teaches us to recognize the true enemy behind such attacks and instructs us on how to fight.

In our key verse today, we learned that our fight is not with the obvious, but rather, the unseen and inconspicuous. The problem is that our martial arts skills cannot touch this enemy — so how are we to fight properly?

Let's take a new view on "empty hand" training, for our weapon, the sword of the spirit, cannot be held physically. What is this sword of the spirit, you might ask? Ephesians 6:17 tells us that it is the Word of God. But how do we use such a sword as this?

Study the Bible, and learn God's Word. If you read Matthew, chapter 4, you learn that Jesus used the very same weapon – the Word of God – against satan in the desert. Three times he quoted scripture before the enemy left Him. As always, Jesus was the perfect model of what we should strive to be. So, sharpen those swords of the spirit by getting in the Word, and prepare for your spiritual battles just as much as you do your physical ones!

Use the space below to add your thoughts, experiences, and convictions to make this message more personal for your audience.

Day 19: God's #1

Key verse(s): Exodus 20:3
"You shall have no other gods before me."

Can someone tell me what an idol is? How about what an idol looks like?
In Old Testament times, idols were often carved images that people were either praying to, showing allegiance to, or worshipping in place of the one true God.
But did you know that not all idols are something physical? The word "idol" has 3 main definitions:

1 – an image used as an object of worship
2 – a false god
3 – one that is adored, often blindly or excessively

In other words, anything that takes the place of your God is an idol. Anything that you devote your life to or love more than God, is an idol. That opens the door up quite a bit more, doesn't it?
Looked at in that light, nearly anything can be an idol if you let it. Love of money can be an idol just as much as Nebuchadnezzar's statue was. Love of yourself over God is also one that people may struggle with. But how about this one – love of sports or activities? If you think about it, if you spend all of your time doing a particular activity (for yourself, as opposed to using your talents for the Kingdom), that very thing can be an idol.
This brings us to a crossroads moment, and I have an important question for you. How many of you spend just as much time in the word as you do on this mat?
How many of you carve out time for God, giving Him the first fruits of your time, just as you do for this class?
This is a hard question, and it may be convicting for some of you. If you feel that the Holy Spirit is tugging at your heart right now, it may be time to reprioritize your daily investments. God should always come first, as you can see in today's key verse. Family should come second. And everything else, you can shuffle around after the first two. But what is most important is that you give the best of yourself to the One who supplies your every breath. If you do that, your faithfulness will produce a fruit you never knew possible.

Use the space below to add your thoughts, experiences, and convictions to make this message more personal for your audience.

Day 20: Muscle Memory

Key verse(s): Hebrews 5:14
"But solid food is for the mature, who by constant use have trained themselves to distinguish good from evil."

We use the term muscle memory a lot in our martial arts classes, but can someone explain what muscle memory really is?

Muscle memory is when you train repetitively long enough that your body can begin to do the same movements without you giving it much thought at all.

What is a great example of how you use your muscle memory in this class?

(Katas, Self-Defense drills, One-Step drills, etc.).

It's great to have that muscle memory in a real-life scenario where you may need to use your martial arts skills, right? Because if you are caught off guard, your adrenaline may spike, causing you to essentially forget what you know. But guess what? Your muscles will still remember what to do if you've practiced enough.

But what about applying that muscle memory to our spiritual life? Our key verse today tells us we can train ourselves in discernment of good and evil. But much like our physical training, we have to train that spiritual muscle constantly if we are going to be able to use it effectively.

One sure-fire way to train your eyes and heart in discernment is by looking at the spiritual fruits of those around you. Matthew 7:15-17 gives us a great start:

"Watch out for false prophets. They come to you in sheep's clothing, but inwardly they are ferocious wolves. By their fruit you will recognize them. Do people pick grapes from thornbushes, or figs from thistles? Likewise, every good tree bears good fruit, but a bad tree bears bad fruit."

Sometimes we need to see beyond what is right in front of us, and we need to hear the intent behind the words you hear. We need that discerning muscle to be in tip top shape so that our muscle memory kicks in when our mind is off guard. Remember this, and you will be ready to move on from spiritual milk to greater things.

Use the space below to add your thoughts, experiences, and convictions to make this message more personal for your audience.

Day 21: Practice Makes Permanent

Key verse(s): Colossians 3:23
"Whatever you do, work at it with all your heart, as working for the Lord, not for human masters."

Raise your hand if you gave today's class 80% of your effort. How about 90%? Did anyone give 100%? Ok, one last question: who gave 110% effort into today's class? Guess what? I can tell who gave their best and who didn't. But why is this important?

Firstly, remember when we talked about muscle memory? That our muscles will do what we practice, regardless of whether we remember in our mind what to do or not? Well, here's a problem with that. If you practice at 50% your best each week in class, that's what your muscles will do if you ever need to use your skills. But if you give, say 100% in every class, that's what your muscles will deal back out if you need to rely on your training.

There is, however, a greater lesson in all of this, and that is found in today's key verse. We should be doing everything as if we are doing it for the Lord. Wow! That's hard to do!

Be honest, how many of you imagine that you are doing your chores for the Lord each day? How many give your homework the same effort you would give Jesus if He asked you to do it? Here's one that's very important: if Jesus was in this room all throughout class today, would you have given the same effort, or would you have tried just a bit harder?

Students, here's the part that's hard for you to grasp. He *was* in class today. If you look at the last part of Joshua 1:9, it states, "…the Lord your God will be with you wherever you go." And knowing this, it even makes me think I could have done better. Who else feels the same?

What I want you all to take away today is that regardless of what you apply yourself to, I want you to remember that you are doing it more for Jesus than anyone else. Jesus, who gave all of Himself for us, not even sparing His own life. Keep that in mind always, and that perspective should always shape your desire and effort to do your best.

Use the space below to add your thoughts, experiences, and convictions to make this message more personal for your audience.

Day 22: Shine Bright

Key verse(s): 1 Timothy 4:12
"Don't let anyone look down on you because you are young, but set an example for the believers in speech, in conduct, in love, in faith, and in purity."

How many of you are 10 or younger? How about 12 and younger? Raise your hands and tell me of something great you have accomplished so far. (Allow students to answer)

How come not all of you raised your hands? Is it because you think you are too young? Can't kids do amazing things as well? Let's look in the Bible at a few examples where kids did miraculous things:

- A while back, we learned how a kid named David defeated a giant Philistine soldier in the book of 1 Samuel.
- In the book of Exodus, you can read about a girl named Miriam, who protected her baby brother, who grew up to be Moses. Many years later, Moses led the Israelites out of their enslavement in Egypt.
- In the book of 2 Kings, there was a boy named Josiah, who was only 8 years old when he became the king of Judah. Even though he was very young, he allowed God to guide him during his 31-year reign, and he was able to influence neighboring countries to reject idols and renew their covenant with the Lord.
- In John 6, there is a story about a boy who faithfully shared his 2 fish and 5 loaves of bread for Jesus to split among a crowd of 5,000. Jesus was able to use this act of faith to perform a miracle that fed the multitude.

Still feel like you can't do great things for the Lord? How about your talents as martial artists? How could you use your God-given talents for His Kingdom?

Did you know that God can even use your martial arts skills for His glory? Each of you has a story to tell, and I can't wait to see how you tell it. Today, I want you all to remember that if one boy's lunch could feed thousands, your talents, however small, can be used in a big, big way – even if you're just a kid.

Use the space below to add your thoughts, experiences, and convictions to make this message more personal for your audience.

Day 23: Face Your Fears!

(Please note that this devotion is more applicable to do at the beginning of class and on a day that you plan to work on board breaking. You can move this devotion according to your existing class plans.)

Key verses: Joshua 1:9
"Have I not commanded you? Be strong and courageous. Do not be afraid; do not be discouraged, for the Lord your God will be with you wherever you go."

How many of you have a fear of something? Let's be honest, everyone is afraid of something, whether you see it or not.

How many of you are afraid, or nervous when it is time for you to test for your next belt rank? How many of you are afraid when you have to spar someone much bigger than yourself? Were any of you scared when you attended your first karate class?

How about this one—how many of you are afraid of breaking boards? If you've never broken a board before, you may not know things like "will it hurt?", "what if I don't break it right away?", or even "what if I try my best and still can't do it?" These are valid concerns, and imagine how someone might feel if they aren't breaking wood, but concrete instead! *That* can be nerve-racking!

In the book of Joshua, you can read a story about the Israelites coming to take possession of the promised land. Now the Israelites had just spent 40 years wandering in the desert because the first time they came to this land, they were too afraid to go into it. And unfortunately, their lack of faith cost them dearly, for their generation missed out on a wonderful opportunity to live a life of blessings God had in store for them. The new generation, however, was ready to end their life of wandering and settle in this fruitful land. Despite logistical challenges (and the land being inhabited already!), the Israelites faced their fears and had to take an "all or nothing" approach to obeying God and their new leader.

Students, that's exactly how it is with breaking your boards—it is an all or nothing approach that depends solely on your ability to look past what is right in front of you and see the rewards of having that faith and courage.

Ready to give that break a try? You got this!

Use the space below to add your thoughts, experiences, and convictions to make this message more personal for your audience.

Day 24: Water Break!

Key verse(s): John 4:14
"..but whoever drinks the water I give them will never thirst. Indeed, the water I give them will become in them a spring of water welling up to eternal life."

Ok everyone, who is ready for a water break? Water breaks are such a wonderful thing, especially if you have been working really hard. Sometimes you just get so thirsty, and I know you are just waiting for me to call out water break, right?

Did you know that there is more than one type of thirst? Sure, you all know your body can get thirsty, your mouth gets all dry, and sometimes you have to cough, and what helps that? Water!

But there is another type of thirst, and that is spiritual thirst. Did you know your spirits need water too? But what kind of water could you give to your spirit? It's not like you could pour water all over your insides, and would that even work anyway? Of course not!

Did you know that one of Jesus' names is the Living Water? Why is that? The answer has to do with our spirits needing water, but we already talked about regular water, and that isn't it. What our spirits need is living water, and that can only come from Jesus.

Let's reread our key verse for today. Jesus promises that when your spirit is thirsty, He is the living water that your spirit needs. His word, His direction, His love, and everything else in between. Not only is He the living water that we need, but if we give our spirits this living water, we will never again thirsty. Does that mean you read the Bible once in a blue moon and call it good? No, it is something you get to drink freely of whenever you want, and the overflow does what? (Hint, look at our key verse)

It becomes a spring of water welling up to eternal life. That sounds a lot more satisfying than our quick few-minute water breaks, doesn't it? So, whenever I call out water break time, I want you to think not only about the physical water you are giving your body, but also the Living Water that your soul needs as well. And if you are feeling thirsty, get a big glass of water and dig into the Word!

Use the space below to add your thoughts, experiences, and convictions to make this message more personal for your audience.

Day 25: The Fruit Of The Spirit

Key verse(s): Galatians 5:22-23
"But the fruit of the Spirit is love, joy, peace, forbearance, kindness, goodness, faithfulness, gentleness and self-control. Against such things there is no law."

If I wanted to look at everyone in this classroom and tell pretty quickly how much each of you know – or what milestones you have already surpassed, how would I be able to tell?

I would look at your belts, of course! As you all know, each of you is given a new belt when you passed the criteria necessary to be considered your next rank, and that tells myself and other instructors what you already know – and what you need to learn next. That makes it pretty easy, doesn't it?

But what if I wanted to take a quick look and see how much you know from the Bible? Is there a rank system for how much you know about God's Word? Unfortunately, there isn't. But there is one way to tell who has been doing their Scriptural homework, so to speak, and today's key verses helps give me guidelines much in the same way your belt color does. The only difference is, I can't use my eyes in the same way. I have to look inside you to see your actions, see your reactions, see your willingness to learn and take instruction, and even see how you treat others and yourself. I have to pay closer attention and look, not for a rank color, but for the presence of very special markers mentioned in our key verses for today.

What am I looking for, you might ask? Let's look again: love, joy, peace, forbearance (patience and forgiveness), kindness, goodness, faithfulness, gentleness, and self-control

Did you all pay attention to the Bible verse? All of these things are considered "a" fruit, not "fruits". If you are getting in the Word, and putting God's words into practice, you will begin to display ALL of the above character traits, not one or some of them. Now, we all start at different places, don't we? And we would be wise to remember Romans 3:10:

"As it is written: There is no one righteous, not even one."

So we can't expect perfection – ever. But we can expect to see the beginnings of that fruit, and the fruit growing in that person. And with much work and spiritual training, you may even have a beautiful harvest one day.

Use the space below to add your thoughts, experiences, and convictions to make this message more personal for your audience

Day 26: Class Rules

Key verse(s): Leviticus 22:31
"Keep my commands and follow them. I am the Lord."

No doubt there are many rules in your martial arts school, and there are many reasons for those rules. Some of them are to keep you safe, some keep others safe, some preserve the safety, cleanliness, and order of the dojo, and some are there as a show of respect to your instructor and fellow classmates.

For the same reasons, God has given us set instructions on how to live our lives, and if we look in the book of Exodus, we can see what God has to say about how we are to live our lives:

Commandment One: You shall have no other gods before God – Exodus 20:3
Commandment Two: You shall not make or worship graven images – Exodus 20:5
Commandment Three: You shall not take God's name in vain – Exodus 20:7
Commandment Four: Remember the Sabbath day by keeping it holy– Exodus 20:8
Commandment Five: Honor your father and mother – Exodus 20:12
Commandment Six: You shall not murder – Exodus 20:13
Commandment Seven: You shall not commit adultery – Exodus 20:14
Commandment Eight: You shall not steal – Exodus 20:15
Commandment Nine: You shall not bear false witness (lie) – Exodus 20:16
Commandment Ten: You shall not covet – Exodus 20:17

As you can see, many of these rules are intended to show respect and honor to our Lord, to keep us and others safe, and to guide you in the paths of righteousness.

One thing you should all take away from today's mat time is that God's rules are supremely more important than the rules in this dojo. If you are able to obey our rules, you are doubly accountable to follow the rules of our Creator.

Please take the time to read and memorize these commandments in your spare time, for the best way to obey is to be aware of what you need to be doing (or not doing). And as Jesus said in John 14:15, "If you love me, you will keep my commandments."

Use the space below to add your thoughts, experiences, and convictions to make this message more personal for your audience

Day 27: The Narrow Gate

Key verse(s): Matthew 7:13-14
"Enter through the narrow gate. For wide is the gate and broad is the road that leads to destruction, and many enter through it. But small is the gate and narrow the road that leads to life, and only a few find it."

Have you ever tried a self-defense technique, but your strike was just an inch or two off from your target? What happened? Were you able to break free or not? How about pressure points? Have you ever tried to do a pressure point on someone, and you were off just half an inch? Did it work? That's one of the challenges of using certain techniques — they require precision accuracy in where you are striking to get the desired effect. Just a hair to the left or right, and your efforts may be for nothing. That small distance could be the difference between victory and defeat.

In today's verse, we learn that it is the same way with our salvation. In the book of Matthew, Jesus is telling us that there are many different paths that can lead to our eternal destruction, but there is only a narrow gate that we can go through to reach eternity with Him. Jesus further encourages us to take that narrow gate, despite the fact that it is likely the least popular way.

What is this narrow gate? Can anyone answer this question?

If you're struggling, fear not. Jesus has an answer to that question in John 14:6:

"I am the way and the truth and the life. No one comes to the Father except through me." Jesus *is* this narrow gate, and the only Way in which we can attain eternity in the presence of God. This is good news! There are many traps along the way, including legalistic thinking, feelings of salvation by heritage, thoughts of salvation by church attendance and membership, salvation by works mentality, predestination ideas, universalism, and so many more. Sometimes, we make things more complicated than they really are, and unfortunately, this is a big area where that happens. Remember, many roads lead to destruction…

If someone had a gift for you, would you have to work for it to earn it? Would you have to pay the person back? Would you only be offered this gift if you were "perfect"? Of course not! Jesus' gift *is* the narrow gate, and it is given to us freely. We need only seek Him to have it.

Use the space below to add your thoughts, experiences, and convictions to make this message more personal for your audience

Day 28: Stone of Help

Key verse(s): 1 Samuel 7:12
"Then Samuel took a stone and set it up between Mizpah and Shen. He named it Ebenezer, saying, "Thus far the Lord has helped us."

Biblically speaking, Ebenezer means "stone of help." In the book of Samuel, we learn that the Philistines were surrounding the Israelites with the plan of engaging them in battle. But despite their numbers, they never had a chance. Do you know why? Because the Lord was watching over the Israelites and protecting them. He made the thunder roar so loud that the Philistines panicked and began to withdraw. It was in their escape efforts that the Israelites pursued, attacked, and defeated their enemies. To commemorate this victory, Samuel took a stone and set it up as a visual reminder of the Lord's help.

What are some things that the Lord has helped you with in this class? Has He given you the gift of strength or flexibility? Has He given you courage on your test day? Has He given you a sense of peace during a big tournament?

Regardless of whether or not you see His hand in your life, the Lord is guiding and protecting you. He is equipping you to prosper, and He is guiding your steps. But all too often, we forget that and assume all that we accomplish comes from our own efforts. So, today's devotion comes with a challenge for you all.

Do any of you have a belt rack at home that you display your belts on? Or how about a board that you have broken and saved? How about test sheets that you keep together? This week's "homework", so to speak, is to write 1 Samuel 7:12 on as many of these things as you can to remind yourself that all of these accomplishments came with the help of the Lord. If you have a belt rack, you can write the verse next to each belt that you earned. On a board, write it across the two broken pieces. On test sheets, write it somewhere that you will see it so that every time you look at what you have done so far it is a reminder that 1) you had the Lord's help, and 2) if He has helped you so far, he will faithfully do so in challenges to come.

Like the Israelites remembering what God has done every time they look at the Ebenezer, you, too, will be reminded of the great things that can come with God on your side.

Use the space below to add your thoughts, experiences, and convictions to make this message more personal for your audience

Day 29: God's Masterpiece

Key verse(s): Ephesians 2:10
"For we are God's handiwork, created in Christ Jesus to do good works, which God prepared in advance for us to do."

Have you ever thought about all of the amazing things God created our bodies to be able to do? In this class, we see just a small fraction of them, but nonetheless, it is awe-inspiring.

We can do high kicks, strong punches, snapping strikes, board breaks, spirited yells, and we can push ourselves farther than we sometimes think we can go. We can keep time with each other, we can be self-motivators, we can learn kata and self-defense, and sometimes, with a LOT of practice, we can even defend ourselves with our eyes closed. (But please don't try that on your own).

Do you think all of these amazing abilities happened by chance? Is it all a coincidence? Of course not!

In today's verse, we learn that we are God's handiwork, and every bit of "you" is intentionally, meticulously, and carefully constructed by loving hands.

Think about this: the God of the universe, who made the skies and seas, who made all of the animals, flowers, growing things, seasons, mountains, valleys and more thought, "now this world needs YOU (point to each student as you say this), and you, and you." Does that make you feel special? You should. Each of us is a miracle, one in which God created for a purpose.

What is that purpose?

Perhaps you have an idea now, and maybe not. But that's ok. Look again at today's verse: created in Christ Jesus to do good works, which God prepared in advance for us to do." You may not know what God's plan is for you yet, but guess what? He does. He knew when He created you, and rest assured, you don't need super powers to do it. You need only to be obedient to His voice when you hear him calling.

God has amazing plans for each one of us, and I can't wait to see what you all accomplish for Him one day!

Use the space below to add your thoughts, experiences, and convictions to make this message more personal for your audience

Day 30: Attitude of Gratitude

Key verse(s): Luke 17:17-18
"Jesus asked, "Were not all ten cleansed? Where are the other nine? Has no one returned to give praise to God except this foreigner?"

In Luke 17:11-19, we read that there were ten men who had leprosy and desperately called out to Jesus as he traveled by. They asked Him to have pity on them and their disease.

You see, leprosy was no joke in Biblical times. People with leprosy not only had the disease to deal with, but they were ostracized and considered unclean to the rest of the population. So until someone with leprosy was healed and cleansed, they could not live a decent life, surrounded by loved ones. Nor could they expect help from anyone else.

Still, Jesus told them that to heal themselves, they were to go to the priests. (Spoiler alert: this was a test of faith. Jesus was the true healer). All of the men did as Jesus told them and were healed, and yet, only one of them found Jesus to thank him for this life-giving miracle. In verse 17, Jesus asks the one that returned to show gratitude, "Were not all ten cleansed? Where are the other nine? Has no one returned to give praise to God except this foreigner?"

The moral of this story is that it is of upmost importance to show gratitude to those that have invested in you some way. Parents, teachers, friends, siblings, and so many others that share their time, talents, instruction, guidance, wisdom, and education with you deserve the courtesy of a thankful attitude. As we see in today's key verse, even our Savior himself was frustrated that out of the nine, only one returned to give Him a proper thank you. And what Jesus did was a life-changing experience for these afflicted men.

My question to all of you this week is this: If you were one of the ten, would you be one of the nine that went about their way without showing gratitude — or would you be the one that went out of his way to humbly show his thanksgiving? We must always strive to be the latter.

Use the space below to add your thoughts, experiences, and convictions to make this message more personal for your audience

Day 31: Sacred Space

Key verse(s): 1 Corinthians 6:19-20
"Do you not know that your bodies are temples of the Holy Spirit, who is in you, whom you have received from God? You are not your own; you were bought at a price. Therefore honor God with your bodies.

Let's talk about our workout space today. We have special rules in the dojo like: no shoes on the mat, no horseplay, no misusing the equipment, bowing in and out, and so many more. Why is that?

Our school is a place where you come to learn physical moves and internal self-control, and so our space is very special. And because of this, we need to show it the proper respect and model the same behavior for other students.

Did you know God's hold temple was very similar? In the book of 2 Chronicles, we learn that Solomon built God's first temple on Mount Moriah. This temple had special rules on how to enter and exit the space, requirements for burnt offerings, cleansing rituals, specifications on what tools could or could not be used (and how to use them), and so much more! There was even an inner room called the Most Holy Place that was off limits to EVERYONE except the Israelite High Priest — and even then, he was only allowed to enter once a year on Yom Kippur. God's temple was not to be taken lightly – it was His holy dwelling place!
And it was up to the Israelites to keep it ritually clean, in proper order, and in a constant state of holiness.

But after Jesus' death, things changed a bit for His believers. In today's key verses, Paul is telling readers that their bodies are the new temples of the Holy Spirit, and that we are not our own. His message is a powerful reminder that we need to treat our bodies with the same respect and care that the Israelites did with their temples.

But how do we "honor God" with our bodies? We do not misuse them. We take care of them by eating right and staying away from things that would hurt our bodies. We keep them clean and in a constant state of readiness to serve the Lord. We keep our hearts and mind clean, and we encourage others to do the same. When you think about how to honor your body as a temple of the Holy Spirit, remember how the Israelites treated their Holy Temple, and strive to do the same.

Use the space below to add your thoughts, experiences, and convictions to make this message more personal for your audience

Day 32: I Can't Do It!

Key verse(s): Jonah 3:3
"Jonah obeyed the word of the Lord and went to Nineveh."

Have you ever been asked to do something in class that you didn't think you could do? Maybe you thought it was too hard, or impossible altogether, or maybe you just didn't feel like putting the effort in. In our lesson today, we turn to the book of Jonah where we learn about a man who was given a task by God to go to an evil city, Nineveh, and warn the inhabitants that judgement was coming.

Jonah didn't care for this command too much. Maybe he was scared to go, thinking he couldn't do what God asked of him. Maybe he had a defiant nature. Or maybe he was just plain lazy. But as we see in this story, not having that faith in yourself can cost you dearly — and sometimes it robs you of a blessing God may have had in store for you.

Instead of going to Nineveh, Jonah boarded a boat to go far away from the city he hated. And while on the ship, there was a terrible storm that had everyone fearing for their lives. Skip ahead a bit, and Jonah admits that his disobedience brought this storm on, and that the other men needed to throw him overboard. Once he was in the sea, he got swallowed up by a fish for 3 days! But God was still protecting Jonah, despite what he had done, and in this time, Jonah repents. The fish threw him up alive (EWWWW!), and thankfully, Jonah learned his lesson. So when God told him again to go to Nineveh, guess what he did? Yep, he obeyed. And miraculously, after his warning, the people of Nineveh repented!

What I want you to all take away from today's lesson is that we may not always feel like listening – for various reasons. But even the hardest tasks come with rewards that we may not have realized, and we have to have faith that our efforts will grow us in a way that make us closer to the person God wants us to be. We may not have to worry about big fish swallowing us up, but that shouldn't distract us from the fact that we need to give our best effort in all that we do, regardless of how challenging it may be.

This week, let's turn our "I cant's!" into "I'll try my best!"

Use the space below to add your thoughts, experiences, and convictions to make this message more personal for your audience

Day 33: Listen Up!

Key verse(s): John 10:27
"My sheep listen to my voice; I know them, and they follow me."

For today's mat time, I want everyone to close their eyes. I will give you a command, and let's see if you think you should follow it. (Give your students a command you usually give them that does not involve moving around). Okay, here's another one – have a parent that you prepared in advance to give a command.

Did everyone follow the command? Why or why not? Was it because you didn't recognize the voice?

This brings up a very good point for you all. In John 10:14-15, Jesus says, "I am the good shepherd; I know my sheep and my sheep know me – just as the Father knows me and I know the Father – and I lay down my life for the sheep."

In this verse, Jesus is saying that those who know Him know His voice. Did you all know the second voice that gave you a command? And did that give you hesitation on whether or not to obey the command?

But how, exactly do we know Jesus' voice? I'll give you a hint: 1 Corinthians 14:33 says this: "For God is not a God of disorder but of peace – as in all the congregations of the Lord's people."

Have you ever been told something that left you shaken, doubtful, worried, or scared? That voice probably did not come from the Good Shepherd then. Have you ever been told something that left you feeling hopeful, comforted, joyful, or excited? How about peaceful? How did you feel about that?

Did you know that sheep really do know the voice of their shepherd? I'm sure if you ask your parents to find one for you, there are countless videos online that depict strangers giving commands to sheep who do not listen to the voice. But once they hear their shepherd, they all go running to him.

Jesus is the Good Shepherd who would never abandon his flock. Who is his flock? You, and me, and everyone else who knows and loves Him. It is our job to learn His voice so that we cannot be misled, and to do that, we have to get in His Word. Like a friend you get to know better the more time you spend with them, we must do the same with our Lord.

Use the space below to add your thoughts, experiences, and convictions to make this message more personal for your audience

Day 34: Sensei Knows

Key verse(s): Revelation 2:19
"I know your deeds, your love and faith, your service and perseverance, and that you are now doing more than you did at first."

We know it is a show of respect by refraining from asking your instructor to test, don't we? When students ask to test, it shows impatience and a lack of faith that your instructor knows if you are ready or not.

Look at today's verse — Jesus is saying that he knows our deeds, love, faith, service, and perseverance. He has His eyes on us always.

Your instructor is very much the same in this dojo. We know how hard you are working when we see you in class each week, and we know if you have been practicing because you look more confident, balanced, and strong. We know when you can remember your kata on your own — or if you are having to look to your neighbor every couple minutes. We know if your body is conditioned by the way you warm up, and whether you can continue your warm up without losing steam. Your instructor knows.

Your instructor also knows what your attitude is like — we may even know your motivation for wanting the belt. Is it because you want the bragging rights, or is it because you legitimately worked hard to earn that honor? We look at those things, too.

Your job as the student is to be patient. When your sensei knows that you are ready, we will let you know. But until then, asking to test, or even worse - nagging, is not showing us that you are ready. It shows that you probably need a little more time to learn perseverance and patience, and it makes us hesitant to promote you.

In the same way, you should all be mindful of your motivations as well. Remember in James 1:3-4, the Bible says, "because you know that the testing of your faith produces perseverance. Let perseverance finish its work so that you may be mature and complete, not lacking anything."

What you learn during this process will only help you in the future, so it is best to learn it now, rather than later. Instead of asking, "why do I have to wait", you should instead ask, "what can I learn while I wait."

Use the space below to add your thoughts, experiences, and convictions to make this message more personal for your audience

Day 35: Great Job!

Key verse(s): 1 Thessalonians 5:11
"Therefore encourage one another and build each other up, just as in fact you are doing."

Have you ever come into karate class feeling down about something that happened at school? Maybe you had an argument with a friend, or you got a bad grade. Maybe you just wanted to be somewhere else rather than working hard in class? Or maybe you didn't get enough time to practice, and you didn't want to look like you hadn't practiced in front of the other students.

Today's key verse reminds us that the space between these walls – and outside of them, should be an all-out challenge for us to step up to and encourage one another, regardless of why we think they may be struggling.

The Bible has a lot to say about encouraging one another. In Proverbs 27:17, it says, "As iron sharpens iron, so one person sharpens another." And in Exodus 17, there is a story of the Israelites battling with the Amalekites. As long as Moses held his hands up with his staff in them, the Israelites would be victorious. But if he dropped his hands, the enemies would start to gain ground.

What happened when Moses grew tired and started to drop his hands? His comrades "sharpened him". Aaron and Hur brought him a stone to sit on, and they physically held his hands up for him so that he remained steady until the Israelites won.

How amazing is that?

It is a beautiful depiction of how we should be supporting one another during times of weakness, exhaustion, and feelings of doubt. But here's the catch: to know that someone needs support, we need to be proactive and intentional about reaching out to them, even if they don't come right out and say they feel that way.

I know that you would be very grateful to have that encouragement if you needed it, so let's challenge ourselves to do the same for others in a great way.

Use the space below to add your thoughts, experiences, and convictions to make this message more personal for your audience

Day 36: Choose Wisely

Key verse(s): 1 Corinthians 15:33
"Do not be misled: "Bad company corrupts good character."

Do you have any friends in school, in sports, or even in this dojo that make bad choices? Some people do that by accident, or just once in a while, and I don't mean people like that. I mean people who do it all...the...time. And on purpose.

Maybe they have a following of "friends" that think that is cool, and maybe one of them has tried to convince you to do something you know is wrong too.

Today's verse reminds us that choosing this type of company will only do you harm. It tells us that your good character will be corrupted — can anyone tell me what that means?

You see, corruption can be a tricky thing. It can be disguised as something else – "cool", "popular", "being a daredevil", and more. And it usually happens over time. That means it's harder to spot it happening right away until like an infection, you might wake up one day and realize just how far it's gotten — and how much harder it will be to repent and turn away from it.

Want a hint?

Most parents can tell when you are hanging out with "the wrong crowd" a lot faster than you can. That's why it is so important to also listen to the wisdom of your parents and elders.

Proverbs 13:20 also reiterates this lesson: "Walk with the wise and become wise, for a companion of fools suffers harm."

Who wants to be wise? Then walk with the wise! Don't fall into bad choices simply because you are surrounded by people who do the same. You have a choice in your character, the company you keep, and the way you handle temptation to stray from the narrow path. And you will never regret taking the right path, for on it, God has blessings just waiting for you that you may never know.

Use the space below to add your thoughts, experiences, and convictions to make this message more personal for your audience

Day 37: Word To The Wise

Key verse(s): Proverbs 15:32
"Those who disregard discipline despise themselves, but the one who heeds correction gains understanding."

Ok students, raise your hands if any of these questions apply to you:

- I asked you to fix your ready hand today
- I had you adjust your stance
- I told you to snap your kick more, or kick higher
- I wanted you to target your hand techniques better
- I addressed your attitude in class
- I corrected the way you were holding your hands up

Whew! That's a lot of corrections, right? Now, raise your hand one final time if you enjoyed being corrected? Not so many hands, I see. I wonder why that is?
Is it because you don't like to be put on the spot? Is it because you thought you were doing it correctly? Or maybe it is because you knew better, and you were just frustrated that you had slipped back into bad habits while practicing?
Regardless of the reason, today's key verse tells us that if we disregard discipline — that is, we don't listen to correction — you have despise for yourself. But if you heed correction (that is, listen to it and take it seriously), then you gain understanding.
What kind of understanding can you gain from some of the things I mentioned above?
Maybe you can learn how to be a better martial artist. Maybe you can see that wisdom doesn't always come from our own mind. Maybe it keeps you from hurting yourself. Whatever the reason, we need to understand that correction most often comes from those who mean the best for you. Your parents, your teachers, and even myself. We want to help you to become the best version of "you" that you can become. And to do that, we are sharing our wisdom and experience with you to help you on that journey.
Next time you are corrected in class, remember today's key verse. Instead of having a sour attitude, reply with a "yes sir!" Or "yes ma'am!"

Use the space below to add your thoughts, experiences, and convictions to make this message more personal for your audience

Day 38: What's In A Name?

Key verse(s): Isaiah 9:6
"For to us a child is born, to us a son is given, and the government will be on his shoulders. And he will be called Wonderful Counselor, Mighty God, Everlasting Father, Prince of Peace."

Students, what are some names you have called me by in this class? Sensei? (Mr./Ms. _____)? Teacher? Instructor? There are many names I can go by, but I only have one real name, given to me by my parents. It is _____. What about all of you? Can a few of you tell me your full names?

Names are very interesting things. It's one of the most important things people need to know us by, but it doesn't say anything about *who* we are inside. Are we good people? Caring, wise, athletic, smart, kind, tall, studious, or even patient? No one would know by your name, would they?

I know someone who has several names, and many of them describe His character. Let's take a look at some of these:

The Alpha and Omega – the beginning and the end
The Author and Finisher of our faith
The Bread of Life
The Chief Cornerstone
The Good Shepherd
The Horn of Salvation
Immanuel – God with us
The King of the Jews
The Lamb of God/ The Son of God
The Light of the World
The Lord of Lords/The King of Kings
Messiah
The Prince of Peace
The Resurrection and Life

And so many more! What do these names tell us about Jesus? (Allow feedback) Next time you think about your name and what it means, think about Jesus and ALL of the names He has – and what they mean. That reminds us just how important and necessary He really is to all of us.

Use the space below to add your thoughts, experiences, and convictions to make this message more personal for your audience

Day 39: Power Up!

Key verse(s): Isaiah 40:29
"He gives strength to the weary and increases the power of the weak."

Who came to class today pumped and ready to go? Who felt tired and would rather be at home? Was your tiredness physical, or was it emotional? Maybe you had a bad day, and working out is the last thing you wanted to do?

Today's key verse is good news! Isaiah is telling us that we don't always have to supply our own energy to accomplish our goals. In fact, we have an endless supply of replenishing energy from our Lord!

Have you ever had a day when you felt like doing nothing? But then you went to church, or maybe you put on some worship music, or maybe you even prayed—and then you felt rejuvenated? Think it can't happen? Try it!

Philippians 4:13 tells us, "I can do all this through him who gives me strength."
How much can you do through Jesus? (ALL this) Because why? (He gives me strength)

Can you get strength from eating well? Yes!
Can you get strength from consuming sugar? Yes, but that's not a healthy way to get energy, is it?
How about this—can you get energy from working out? Yes!

But guess what? All those things eventually leave you feeling tired again—they don't last forever. Much like Jesus being the bread of our spirit and the water of life for our souls, Jesus sustains us in a way that nothing earthly can. And when we have faith in what He can do through us, it allows us to draw on that fountain of youth, so to speak.

Jesus *wants* us to feel our best—He wants us to come to Him for a fill-up. But most of us don't remember to do that. This week, I challenge each of you to seek Jesus when you're having an "off day". See what it does for you, and I would love to hear all about it in our next class!

Use the space below to add your thoughts, experiences, and convictions to make this message more personal for your audience

Day 40: Flesh vs. Spirit

Key verse(s): Romans 12:21
"Do not be overcome by evil, but overcome evil with good."

Today's mat time is packed with truth, so I hope you all are ready for a treat! We are going to talk about our flesh nature verses our spirit nature. We all have two sides that are seemingly warring inside of us all the time. Our spirit wants to do what is right (and the Holy Spirit convicts us if we are straying from that), yet our flesh nature puts up a fight and often wants to do the wrong thing.

Romans 7:19 reiterates this: "For I do not do the good I want to do, but the evil I do not want to do – this I keep on doing." Unfortunately, this a battle that we often lose if we don't have enough self-control.

Galatians 4:9 asks us, "But now that you know God – or rather are known by God – how is it that you are turning back to those weak and miserable forces? Do you wish to be enslaved by them all over again?"

You see, when we accept Jesus into our hearts, we are no longer a slave to sin, and yet, we still make mistakes if we don't continually seek Him and His strength to do what is right. Think about it this way – I'll use dragons because dragons play a very important role in Asian culture. Imagine you have two dragons raging inside of you at all times. One is called Spirit – and the other is called Flesh, and they never stop fighting. Which one will win?

(Answer – the one you feed)

How do you know which one you are feeding? Let's go to Romans 8:5:

"Those who live according to the flesh have their minds set on what the flesh desires; but those who live in accordance with the Spirit have their minds set on what the spirit desires."

That's a LOT of truth! So ask yourselves, which dragon are you feeding? How could you make life choices that will starve the Flesh dragon and allow the Spirit dragon to thrive?

You all have some homework to do this week, and it should start with prayer.

Use the space below to add your thoughts, experiences, and convictions to make this message more personal for your audience

Day 41: Raise a Kiai

Key verse(s): Revelation 19:6-7
"Then I heard what sounded like a great multitude, like the roar of rushing waters and like loud peals of thunder, shouting: "Hallelujah! For our Lord God Almighty reigns. Let us rejoice and be glad and give him glory!..."

Raise your hand if you know what a kiai (or kihap) is. I'll give you a hint — we do it in class all the time. It's our yell! We usually use our kiais (kihaps) when we are attacking, and it has several benefits: it scares our attacker, it lets other people know something is going on, it allows us to compress our diaphragm so that we cannot get winded, it gives us a burst of power, and sometimes just doing it makes us more spirited, excited, and purposeful.

While people in Biblical times didn't do the same thing, they had something that was pretty similar. Know what that was? A Hallelujah. What does "hallelujah" actually mean? It means to be bright, to shine or radiate. It is used to express praise or joy, and it exclaims praise and thanksgiving to God.

Hallelujah is comprised of two Hebrew words joined together:

hillel – praise
jah – Lord

The user of this word would, essentially be radiating praise to God, and in doing so, this would often give them a surge of spiritual power. Sound familiar?

We may not be yelling "hallelujah" in class, but we can be sure that by having this attitude of praise (even when we are kiai'ing in class), we will reap the benefits of having an attitude of praise for our Lord. And like a cold, having that intentional attitude of devotion to God can be very contagious. Imagine if everyone caught that from you! What would this class look like? What would your school look like? What would the world look like?

This week, let's focus our attention to having an attitude of praise, no matter what things look like around us. See what it can do for you — and see what it does for those around you.

Let's close with this verse: "Clap your hands, all you nations; shout to God with cries of joy." (Psalm 47:1)

Use the space below to add your thoughts, experiences, and convictions to make this message more personal for your audience

Day 42: Steak, Anyone?

Key verse(s): Hebrews 5:14
"But solid food is for the mature, who by constant use have trained themselves to distinguish good from evil."

What would you all do if I was testing someone for a yellow belt, and I gave them a brown belt instead? You would probably think that wasn't right – and for good reason. What if I was judging a tournament, and I let the person who got the least points walk away with the first-place trophy? There would be a lot of head scratching (and probably some yelling about it from the stands). Or what if I told someone they were getting a special award, but then gave it to someone else on the day of awarding? Those watching would say all of the above scenarios are "wrong", wouldn't they? Certainly, I wouldn't be acting with integrity, would I? I hope that you would see it that way too.

You see, students, today's key verse reminds us that those who are spiritually mature would see the problems in these situations. Their spiritual glasses are cleaner than others, and this helps them to distinguish between good and evil better than those who do not have the guiding moral compass of The Word. What one person sees as right, another might see as wrong, and what draws that line? I'll give you a hint: it's in a big book we have been learning a lot about. The Bible.

What else does the Bible tell us about spiritual blindness: "But the way of the wicked is like deep darkness; they do not know what makes them stumble." (Proverbs 4:19) And also this: "The person without the Spirit does not accept the things that come from the Spirit of God but considers them foolishness, and cannot understand them because they are discerned only through the Spirit." (1 Corinthians 2:14)

When you are able to tell right from wrong by God's standards, you are ready for "solid food", but when you are still learning what is acceptable and what is not in God's eyes, you are like a baby, needing what nourishes a baby – milk.

So which one of you would rather have a glass of milk over a hot, fresh pizza or a perfectly grilled steak with vegetables?

Bring on the meal for me!

Use the space below to add your thoughts, experiences, and convictions to make this message more personal for your audience

Day 43: Rise Above

Key verse(s): Proverbs 5:22
"The evil deeds of the wicked ensnare them; the cords of their sins hold them fast."

Have you ever been in a headlock before? How about a choke hold, or even a joint lock? It doesn't feel good to be trapped that way, does it? Sometimes you try to think of what you can do to get out of it as fast as possible, but you may not have the proper training to release those grips on you.

Today's verse reminds us that evil deeds can be just as hard to break free of as those grips, and oftentimes, harder. The "cords of sin" hold fast to us, and we may or may not have the spiritual training to break free of them.

What are some of these "sins" that trap us? Bitterness, anger, pride, and even some that we purposefully hold on to, like grudges.

Leviticus 19:18 reminds us, "Do not seek revenge or bear a grudge against anyone among your people, but love your neighbor as yourself. I am the Lord."

The cords of sin can be strong, and they can hold us back from being the best person we can be. But guess what? There is an answer for each scenario that acts like a pair of scissors that you can use to release sin's hold on you. And God knew we would need those scissors! That's why He gave us His Word – because He only wants the best for you. But even more so, He gave us something even better. He gave us His Son, who gave His life for all of us, and the Holy Spirit that helps us in times of trouble. With all of this amazing help, I wonder why we keep falling into the same traps?

Living a life weighed down by sin is no way to live at all. If we want to live a joy-filled life, we have to take a lesson from Hebrews 12:1-3:

1. Throw off everything that hinders and the sin that so easily entangles
2. Run with perseverance the race marked out for us
3. Fix our eyes on Jesus

Then, and only then can we live our lives as fully as God intends for us all.

Use the space below to add your thoughts, experiences, and convictions to make this message more personal for your audience

_____

_____

_____

_____

_____

_____

_____

_____

_____

_____

_____

_____

_____

_____

_____

Day 44: Elbow Grease

Key verse(s): Psalm 126:6
"Those who go out weeping, carrying seed to sow, will return with songs of joy, carrying sheaves with them."

Who loves getting a new belt? Do you love the work that goes into earning that belt?

How about a trophy in a tournament—who likes getting those? Did you love all the extra practice you had to do to earn it?

Did anyone get a special award for good character this year? Was it easy to earn it?

Our key verse today reminds us that it is in our flesh nature to dislike the hard work we have to put in to accomplish great things—but boy do we like the rewards of it! We live in a time where so much is handed to us, but it hasn't always been that way. In Biblical times, for example, people had to toil in the hot sun all day long just to earn enough to eat for a day or two. They didn't have running water, so they had to walk to wells, often far from their homes, carrying large ceramic pots to carry the water home in. And if you wanted a hamburger…don't get me started on that process!

What would happen if those people decided they didn't "feel" like putting in the effort? Here's a hint: it's in 2 Thessalonians 3:10: "For even when we were with you, we gave you this rule: 'The one who is unwilling to work shall not eat.'"

Tough luck! Do people still have this problem today? Some do, in many parts of the world, but where we live, not so much. And I am grateful for that, but at the same time, we have a lot of entitlement issues for all of the advantages we have (and our lack of understanding that there is value in hard work).

God values hard work, and so do I. In our dojo, we work hard for what we want, and we earn our ranks—they are not handed to us. If I taught you that you get to rank up, regardless of whether you know your material or work hard, how would that make you feel about that belt? It wouldn't be worth much, would it?

I want you all to reflect on the value of what you have, and though you may not have worked to earn it, someone else did. Please show gratitude to your family for all they have done for you, and return the favor when they need help.

Use the space below to add your thoughts, experiences, and convictions o make this message more personal for your audience

Day 45: Practice Makes Permanent

Key verse(s): Joshua 1:8
"Keep this Book of the Law always on your lips; meditate on it day and night, so that you may be careful to do everything written in it. Then you will be prosperous and successful."

I hope you all pay close attention to my instruction in each class, but let's just pretend you don't…

What if I tell you to punch like so (demonstrate). But you go home and practice this instead? (demonstrate incorrectly)

What if I tell you to hold your hands like this (demonstrate), but you practice day and night all week like this? (demonstrate incorrectly)

How about katas? What if I teach you the steps, and you practice them backwards? What happens in each of these cases?

This, students, is a hard example of "practice makes permanent".

You have probably heard "practice makes perfect", right? But that's only the case if you practice it correctly every time. More often than not, we have a "practice makes permanent" scenario where a technique was practiced incorrectly so many times that it is harder to unlearn the incorrect way than it was to learn it properly the first time.

Studying the Bible is very much the same. In our key verse today, God is instructing Joshua to 1) keep God's law always on his lips and 2) study it. Did you know you can try to do things the right way as hard as possible, with as much good intention as you can muster – and still get it wrong? Just like in the martial arts, studying God's Word isn't a one-and-done deal. You have to study the Bible, commit it to memory, and practice it all the time if you want to be proficient in its teachings. And as important as martial arts are to me and all of you, knowing God's Word is SO MUCH MORE important.

Let's not let our Biblical training become a "practice makes permanent" blunder. If there is anything worthy of our time and efforts, this should be the highest priority.

Use the space below to add your thoughts, experiences, and convictions to make this message more personal for your audience

Day 46: Hit the Showers!

Key verse(s): 1 Samuel 16:7
"But the Lord said to Samuel, "Do not consider his appearance or his height, for I have rejected him. The Lord does not look at the things people look at. People look at the outward appearance, but the Lord looks at the heart."

If we have a really good workout, how do we look after class? Our uniforms may be dirty and have sweat on them, our hair may be ruffled, our faces are likely sweaty, and let's be honest. We may not smell great either. In fact, if we leave this class in that condition, what do you think other people may think about you?

They might think your personal hygiene isn't great, they might not want to be close to you, and the sad part is, maybe they won't look at you with a lot of respect for having a dirty face. You see, students, the world has a problem with judgement: we tend to judge others on their appearances. Is it right? Of course not—other people have no idea the heart you carry inside you, the good things you've done or the accomplishments you've earned. They didn't see that you helped me clean up after class today, or that you assisted your parents with dinner last night. So it's really an unfair judgement, isn't it?

The good news is that God never looks at us that way. In our key verse today, we are reminded that the Lord looks at our hearts, while the world judges us on our outward appearance. Wouldn't you rather someone look at what's inside than on the outside? I would! But more so, I would want the Creator of the world to look at my heart because there's just no realistic way that I could look perfect on the outside *all* the time, no matter how hard I tried. And He knows that! (Which I'm thankful for).

So if God looks at the inside, and the world looks at the outside, who do you think we should model ourselves after? God, of course!

Is there someone you have been judging on the outside? Maybe they have glasses, or dirty shoes, or a haircut that makes other kids tease them. I bet that person has a lot more going on on the inside than you know. My challenge to all of you this week if to find someone that you feel is being judged from the outside and make an effort to do something kind for them. Try to get to know their heart, and see what comes about from it.

Use the space below to add your thoughts, experiences, and convictions to make this message more personal for your audience

Day 47: The Good Win

Key verse(s): 1 Corinthians 13:4
"Love is patient, love is kind. It does not envy, it does not boast, it is not proud."

Raise your hand if you've ever beat someone in a sparring match. How about if you've placed first place in a tournament? Let's see who's won other sports games? How did it make you feel to win? How did you react when you won?

Did you know that my last question is the most important of all the others? Why is that?

In today's key verse, Paul reminds us that love is not boastful, and it is not proud. We talked about humility already, and pride is the opposite of a humble attitude. Does that mean you can't be proud of yourself if you win? No! Does it mean you can't be happy that you earned something you worked really hard for? No!

It simply means that you should courteously celebrate, and take the other person's feelings into account as well. Here are some scenarios for you, and tell me if you think this is a demonstration of love:

You won a karate match and shook hands with the other person while bowing.
(Yes!)
You placed 2nd place in a kata division of a tournament, and yelled to the 3rd place student, "Ha! I won!"
(No! Of course not!)
How about at school – you win the spelling bee for your grade. You say to the other students who competed, "I won because I'm smarter."
(I don't think that's ok, and I hope you all agree.)

What does love look like in each of these scenarios? Having respect and compassion for the other people who may have worked even harder than you to prepare for said competition, and still didn't win. You can be happy and proud of yourself, but you must, as Peter says in 1 Peter 5:5, "clothe yourselves with humility toward one another, because, "God opposes the proud but shows favor to the humble."

When you are at the top of your game and still show respect for others around you, you can have your cake and eat it too!

Use the space below to add your thoughts, experiences, and convictions to make this message more personal for your audience

Day 48: Zip It!

Key verse(s): James 3:7-8
"All kinds of animals, birds, reptiles and sea creatures are being tamed and have been tamed by mankind, but no human being can tame the tongue. It is a restless evil, full of deadly poison."

How many times have you had a belt exam, and you could hear people talking in the background? Was it distracting to you? Or, how about this one: how many times have you talked during someone else's test?

When you forgot your kata steps, and forgot how to do a specific kick in class, have you had anyone giggle at your mistakes? Have *you* been the one to giggle at other's misfortunes?

Today's verses are a powerful reminder that our tongues need to be tamed much like we would attempt to train a wild animal. In fact, many wild animals have been tamed by humans successfully — but we have yet to learn how to tame our own mouths.

Do you realize the power that lies in the tongue? Proverbs 18:21 expounds on this:

"Death and life are in the power of the tongue, and those who love it will eat its fruits."

Furthermore, Proverbs 13:3 says, "Those who guard their lips preserve their lives, but those who speak rashly will come to ruin."

There are so many more Bible verses that reiterate today's topic, but what you need to take away from our lesson is that you have the power to build others up or tear them down.

With your tongue, you can avoid trouble or get into a lot of it. Let's look at Proverbs 15:1 – "A gentle answer turns away wrath, but a harsh word stirs up anger." With your words, you can choose to glorify God, or you can serve the enemy. That's a lot of responsibility, isn't it?? Does it make you want to think about what you say before you say it just a tad more?

Make no mistake, God encourages all of us, regardless of our age, to attempt to do the nearly-impossible task of using our tongues for good. Even if that means we have to work hard at it for a LONG time, and even if it means letting go of some of our pride in the process. Regardless, it is something we need to strive to do until we have mastered the beast within.

Use the space below to add your thoughts, experiences, and convictions to make this message more personal for your audience

Day 49: Guard Your Treasure

Key verse(s): Matthew 6:19-21
"Do not store up for yourselves treasures on earth, where moths and vermin destroy, and where thieves break in and steal. But store up for yourselves treasures in heaven, where moths and vermin do not destroy, and where thieves do not break in and steal. For where your treasure is, there your heart will be also."

Be honest, who loves to earn a nice, big trophy after a hard competition? Sure, to some degree, I would say nearly all of us do! And winning prizes or awards is not wrong, by any means, but when we take into account *how* we won it, that puts a different spin on it. Here are some things to consider:

1) Did you show good sportsmanship? Did you have a good attitude?
2) Did you seek to glorify God through you, or did you try to set yourself on a pedestal?
3) Did you cheat to gain the earthly prize?
4) Did you slander other competitors? Or were you supportive of them?
5) Did you thank those who helped you to get where you are?

All of these things make for a true winner. Know why? In our key verses today, we are reminded that our earthly treasure will never last. They will fade, break, collect dust, and maybe even get stolen. Those things can be taken from us in a heartbeat. But there are some treasures that cannot be taken from us – not even when we go to be with Jesus. Those are our heavenly treasures - treasures that are completely priceless because they never can fade, break, or be taken away.

Colossians 3:2 reminds us, "Set your minds on things above, not on earthly things." What kinds of things above?

The goodness of the Lord, and the unconditional love that He has for us. The sacrifice He made for all of us so that we could attain something we never deserved. And the opportunity for us to model Him and make this world a brighter place.

As it says in 1 Corinthians 1:31, "Therefore, as it is written: "Let the one who boasts boast in the Lord.""

Use the space below to add your thoughts, experiences, and convictions to make this message more personal for your audience

Day 50: Our Refuge

Key verse(s): Psalm 91:4
"He will cover you with his feathers, and under his wings you will find refuge; his faithfulness will be your shield and rampart."

Have you ever practiced striking drills with a partner, and the only thing between you and their kicks was a body target? Were you scared at all? I bet you were glad to have that padding between the two of you, weren't you? But the problem with body targets, or armor, or anything else that is designed to protect us is that nothing on this earth is foolproof. There is no way any one thing could protect you 1) indefinitely and 2) from anything and everything that may harm you.

It's a good thing we serve a God that is able to protect you indefinitely AND from anything that may harm you! Psalm 46:1 reminds us, "God is our refuge and strength, an ever-present help in trouble." What exactly is a refuge? It is a shelter or protection from danger. How do you think God can be a shelter to us? (Allow students to answer)

Those are some great answers! What's important to remember is that God created this entire world, everything around it, and everything in it. He has the ability, and it is in Him that we must trust. Let's go back into Psalms for a second. Chapter 18:30 says, "As for God, his way is perfect: the Lord's word is flawless; he shields all who take refuge in him."

This week, I want you all to focus on these verses. If you have a worry, give it to God in prayer. If you have a problem, seek His Word and see what the answer is. If you have a joy you want to share, share it with Him! He is our shelter, and we don't only look for shelter when we are in trouble, do we? In fact, all manner of life happens in our earthly shelters – good times, bad, and everything in between.

What we need to remember is that we need to seek refuge in our heavenly refuge just as much as we do our earthly, or we are putting our ultimate faith in the wrong place.

Use the space below to add your thoughts, experiences, and convictions to make this message more personal for your audience

Day 51: Stand Together

Key verse(s): 1 Corinthians 1:10
"I appeal to you, brothers and sisters, in the name of our Lord Jesus Christ, that all of you agree with one another in what you say and that there be no divisions among you, but that you be perfectly united in mind and thought."

Have you ever seen an Olympic martial arts team performing kata in flawless unity down the same half-second? It's really a beautiful thing, and it's just as amazing when you all do your katas to the same time as well. It doesn't happen often, but when it does, it is a sight to behold.

But at times, we get not-so perfect results where some are way off or behind or ahead of others, and it looks more chaotic than anything. In fact, if two students are too close and not looking around, they could hurt each other as well.

Today's key verse reminds us to strive to be in unity – not just for the appearance, but for the good of the body. I wish I could say that churches all over the world agreed the way Paul encouraged us in this message, but the hard fact is that they do not, and there are often disagreements, resentments, arguing, and sadly, anger and malice. As believers, we should be the example, not succumb to the way of the unbeliever, don't you think?

Imagine how our dojo would look if all of you students fought all the time – argued, had physical altercations, and always blamed the others for the chaos that would ensue. It wouldn't be a pretty picture, and unfortunately, that's how the world looks at times. What if it was the other way around? What if we all strived for peace, swallowed our egos, and kept the peace? Quite a different scenario, isn't it?

When we think of those martial arts students performing kata in perfect unity, we can only imagine how wonderful the world would look if believers looked the same in a world that already has enough problems of its own.

This week, let's hold our tongues when we want to bicker, and for the health of humanity, try to find what you have in common with others, rather than finding reasons for division. I think you will be pleasantly surprised at what you can accomplish when you are all on the same page.

Use the space below to add your thoughts, experiences, and convictions to make this message more personal for your audience

Day 52: Line Up!

Key verse(s): Matthew 20:16
"So the last will be first, and the first will be last."

When I call "line up" at the beginning and end of class, what usually happens?

On a good day, everyone runs to line up, double checks their place in line, and holds their ready position until we bow in. On a bad say, there's talking, excessive shifting, students meandering over to line, and others fighting over who goes on which side. So, if we line up according to rank and rage, why argue over who goes where? What's the big importance of being further up the line than your classmate?

In today's verse, Jesus reminds us that those of us who have a mindset of "me first", will ultimately be last in line—while those who have a humble attitude and view others as more important will be considered "first" in line. Jesus considered this humble spirit very important, for later on in chapter 23, verse 12, He reiterates, "For those who exalt themselves will be humbled, and those who humble themselves will be exalted."

Have you ever heard the saying, "pride comes before a fall"? It's very popular, and not-so-surprisingly, accurate. History is riddled with people who encountered "a fall" after demonstrating a level of pride that wins "first place." In fact, in the book of Daniel, chapter 4, you can read about the Babylonian King Nebuchadnezzar, who grew incredibly prideful about his belongings and lifestyle, attributing it to his own greatness and not a gift from God. Nebuchadnezzar's "fall" was the unfortunate punishment of being turned into a beast for seven years. He was driven away from civilization and lived the life of a wild animal until his time of humbling was over.

Skip ahead one more chapter, and you can read about the fall of King Belshazzar, whose pride brought down severe judgement during an elaborate party of his. It was that very night that he was slain, and his entire kingdom was taken over by King Darius of the Medes.

What can we learn from these stories? It would benefit us to adopt an attitude of gratitude and humility before pride gets a foothold in your life. For when it nips at your heel, that fall won't look pretty.

Use the space below to add your thoughts, experiences, and convictions to make this message more personal for your audience

Day 53: Fix "You" First

Key verse(s): Matthew 23:25-26
"Woe to you, teachers of the law and Pharisees, you hypocrites! You clean the outside of the cup and dish, but inside they are full of greed and self-indulgence. Blind Pharisee! First clean the inside of the cup and dish and then the outside also will be clean."

In today's verses, we learn that Jesus, like most of us, had frustration with the hypocrites of His time. What is a hypocrite? Can anyone tell me?

A hypocrite is someone who expects others to behave or do things they would never do themselves. It's as if they can see the flaws in others but are unable to see anything wrong with themselves.

How would you feel if one of the assistant instructors told you to fix your stance if theirs was suffering more often than not? How about if I told you to get your kick to at least belt level, but I only kicked knee level myself (and did so out of laziness, not an injury)? What if someone who never yelled during their katas got on to you about missing a couple of your own? That would be pretty frustrating, wouldn't it? And wouldn't we be tempted to return the critiquing favor back to them?

Matthew 7:5 has more to say about people with a hypocritical nature:

"You hypocrite, first take the plank out of your own eye, and then you will see clearly to remove the speck from your brother's eye."

This verse is, in essence, saying "fix yourself before you tell anyone else that they are broken." And rightly so! Some people feel the need to correct others because of a conviction in their own hearts that they don't want to face — or maybe they seek to elevate themselves by nitpicking others. Some people just don't have anything more constructive to do with their time, and truly, that is to be pitied.

Next time you feel the need to correct someone, ask yourself these things:
-Is your critique helpful?
-Is it there to encourage and build others up?
-Is it there to keep someone safe?
-Does it come from a genuine heart that cares about the other person?

If your answer to any of these is "no", then perhaps you should look in the mirror. You might just have something in your eye!

Use the space below to add your thoughts, experiences, and convictions to make this message more personal for your audience

About The Author

Ginny Aversa Tyler is a wife and homeschooling mother of four children.
She is the owner and founder of DMD Tae Kwon Do, a Christian martial arts school near McKinney, Texas.
(www.dmdtaekwondo.com)

Inspired by the endless lessons both God's Word and the martial arts have to offer, Ginny has written multiple publications so that others can tie their love of the martial arts to the lifelong guidance our Heavenly Father offers in a tangible way for their classrooms, students, and families.

Ginny's passion for teaching, not just her own children and students, is the basis for her books, through which she wishes to inspire children and instructors all over the world to seek Biblical truths outside the walls of their home, school, and martial arts classes.

Other Titles by Ginny Tyler

Kingdom Kicks Series:

A Lesson On Perseverance
A Lesson On Humility
A Lesson On Self-Control
A Lesson On Courtesy
A Lesson On Indomitable Spirit
A Lesson On Integrity
A Lesson On Obedience
A Lesson On Strength
Kingdom Kicks Coloring Book
Lessons From The Mat
A Lesson On Wisdom

Under The Door